To All the Mirrored Doors
of Beginning, a Journey Ending

To All the Mirrored Doors
of Beginning, a Journey Ending

RUTH RIFKA

RESOURCE *Publications* • Eugene, Oregon

TO ALL THE MIRRORED DOORS OF BEGINNING, A JOURNEY ENDING

Copyright © 2024 Ruth Rifka. All rights reserved. Except for brief quotations in critical publications or reviews, no part of this book may be reproduced in any manner without prior written permission from the publisher. Write: Permissions, Wipf and Stock Publishers, 199 W. 8th Ave., Suite 3, Eugene, OR 97401.

Resource Publications
An Imprint of Wipf and Stock Publishers
199 W. 8th Ave., Suite 3
Eugene, OR 97401

www.wipfandstock.com

PAPERBACK ISBN: 979-8-3852-3391-5
HARDCOVER ISBN: 979-8-3852-3392-2
EBOOK ISBN: 979-8-3852-3393-9
VERSION NUMBER 11/19/24

To Our Better Angels and Mentors, Who Travel with Us Along the Way, Inspiring Our Lives with Purpose and Meaning.

Contents

Acknowledgements | ix

The Most Dangerous Animal in the World | 1
The Search Slows Down | 2
Art | 3
Today, I Am a Frightened Old Child | 5
With Every Breath | 7
Living the Answer | 8
To All the Mirrored Doors of Beginning | 9
We Are the Offspring Stardust | 10
Nevertheless | 11
Everything Breathes of God | 12
Education | 13
The Oldest Person in the Room | 14
Lament for the Crucifixions of October 7 | 15
We Are on the Edge of Chaos Again | 17
This Lament Continues | 19
Standing Over One's Own Grave | 20
Sand | 21
What Exactly Are You God? | 23
In a Hymn of Sounding Glory | 24
God's Endless Confession Booth | 25
Standing Near the Edge of Chaos in a Time of War | 26

Remembering My Dark Funk at the Lovely
  Beach on a Perfect Day | 28
Vade Mecum | 29
The Re-Naming of Things | 30
We Are Instructed | 31
How to Die Alone | 32
The Morning Prayer | 33
There is a Candle in the Dark | 34
Does the Divine Sensorium of God | 35
World War Three | 36
The War Against the Jews—Day 86. Israel, Ever
  Startup Nation Built on Ashes | 38
Day 88 | 40
The Hostages. Day 88 of the Unspeakable | 41
These Are the Messages Writing Themselves Out | 42
Lament | 43
Kabbalah | 44
Gnarled Old Tree | 45
Future Evolve | 46
Experimental Flaw | 47
If This is the First Day and the Last Day of My
  Life, How Shall I Proceed? | 49
If This Is the Last Day of My Life, How Shall I Proceed? | 52
If This Is the Last Day | 55
Shoah | 57
Make My Peace | 59
Lou, I Held Your Hand | 60
Last Messages: The Writing on The Wall in a Time of War | 61
In My 96th Year | 62
Full Circle | 64
I Will Go Out Fighting | 67
This War of Wars and More Futile Quarrels with God | 68

From a Dinosaur Evolved a Soaring Bird | 70
All the Journeys' Ends Are New Beginnings | 71
Mashber, The Birthing Stool of Crisis | 72
Old Age Must Live with Not Knowing | 74
Unicursal Labyrinth | 76
IS | 77
Form Returns to Formlessness | 78
The Garden Breathes into Winter | 80

Coda to a Bitter Story Unfolding
PARTING BLESSINGS, AS I LEAVE | 83
How Beautiful the World Could Be. And is. | 85
IF GOD IS IN THE EVERYTHING, AND IS | 86
Tree Artist Has Burst Out Wild and Fast, This June.
  It is Day 261 of War | 87

Glossary | 89

Acknowledgements

With thanks to Bunny Iskov, Founder of The Ontario Poetry Society, for her astute eye and generous mentoring. With thanks to supportive family. With gratitude for my husband Lou, lifelong truest friend, abiding love, and wise advisor. May his memory be for a blessing.

The Most Dangerous Animal in the World

Bronx Zoo. Circa 1963.
I remember that message
at the entrance to the Gorilla House—
spelled out in blood-red block letters
above a hanging mirror:

"You are looking at the most dangerous animal in the world.
It alone of all the animals that ever lived can exterminate
(and has) entire species of animals. Now it has the power
to wipe out all life on earth."

I recognized my image with a jolt
as the caption made its point
regarding my own paltry sins.

Mercifully never having been put to the big test,
I see they pan out kind of tame.
Thank you, God.

But why *is* evil so easy?
Millions wandering, dying, at one man's command,
far too many of us innocent human ants
are trapped in dystopias not of our making,
while Fate's hand keeps writing cryptic messages
on Time's wall, for us to contemplate in guilty dread.

Why was all this dreamed up?

The Search Slows Down

Truths leap out fast.

The porthole of Death lies ahead—
all life's terminating dimension and destination.
Fate's blunt message stamped on our foreheads.

From this universe of parallel truths
we shall leave naked again
as we entered, submerged back
through the portal of all beginnings and endings.

Invited? Welcomed?
A lucky mistake on the path to . . .?

Is the glory and misery
our characters jumping off the pages of God's novel,
or an inchoate story to pass the invention of time?
Somewhere by chance
are finer magical creatures evolved with wings
soaring the heavens,
singing with God
who is constantly becoming
"*I am that I am.*"

Art

I love the dialogues of artists
obsessing deep, deep into art,
art, art with a capital A,
all the uplifting transcendence of it

until I get a vision of meal moths
eating pages of poetry,
and worms corroding canvas,
and Time wiping off all traces of cave art.
When I am reminded
how fervently Nazis lusted after the art they plundered,
and how Wagner would have wished this particular little Jew very dead.

Art is glorious food for the soul,
feeding the very worst of us.

Odd, how I find this a bit of a message from God.
We are not as important as we think we are.
God has the last word as Critic.
Grand Artist, Dramatist Supreme.
Writing down the heavens,
painting us into masterpiece worlds
of transcending exhortations,
around a *tragoida*, a tragedy.
The derivation of which is:
Tragos, goat, plus *oide,* song.
Goat Song.

Was that the original idea?
The keening song of a scapegoat banished into the wilderness,
the tragedy of the necessary victim,
the DNA formulation of life going forward in great drama.

We will never fathom God's blueprint vision—
a certain *Adam Kadmon*,
in God's Image. Primordial Creature.
The mirror for God to see God.

Failed Art to be wiped off
eternity's blackboard of formulas
again and again, until God gets it right?

The Grand Conductor continuing,
master juggler of all the heavens,
keeps all the worlds turning,
mindful, or not, of us.

God beyond definition,
choreographing the dance of life and death.
God, in the everything.
God, One.
Is.

Today, I Am a Frightened Old Child

I woke up from and am still in a puzzling dream, lost, lost.
I have lost my way again and can't get home.
I try to remember the address to order a taxi. And when I do,
it's a place closed off, forbidden. No vehicle travels there.
I must walk along this long road in the hot sun.
I pass a troop of soldiers marching resolved, resilient, purposed,
but they are marching towards me, counter my destination.
Yes, I get it. Everyone will march on after I reach where I am going.

Once, there was pleasure in that place to where I am marching,
but also, a frisson of fear. Portal to Death and Birth I believe,
is its name. This is a mixed-up dream.

I wake up and I understand the meaning.
This is my final journey to the self's fate
I keep searching to understand, make peace with.
I begin the day. The morning paper arrives.
The front page tells the story of the broken children of Ukraine.
O God, I am such an old woman.
Yet, the frightened child in me who can still cry,
haunts me again.

Frida Kablo said, "I want to be inside your darkest everything."
No. No. No. I can't bear that idea. Not me.
How could I choose to be in the shaking souls
of the children of Ukraine
and all the other hellholes allowed to happen?

This earth we occupy and all the things we do—
there are lamentations enough for forever.
A child suffering is the unholiest thing.
What worse sin can we commit?
In my dreams I discover there is some kind of Karma
for some of us. But where is redeeming comfort
for slaughtered innocents?
God, make me a believer again,
because there must be retribution in the end,
and heaven for those who've never sinned.

With Every Breath

we breathe closer to God's
tryst with the soul.
We rejoin to the first
evanescence
in an ever distant
seventh heaven ahead,
wider, wider in the widening spaces,
burrowing into the oneness
that joins.

I am nothing,
and I am the everything too.

Living the Answer

Only one possibility,
live life as an answer to the question
of what is final.

So many iterations of a body
peel away like dead onion skins:
the daily dying,
the daily being re-born,
the morning stranger in the mirror,
foreign as the ones
posing smiling in
the stacked photo albums
documenting . . . whose life exactly?

Enigma keeps writing a new face,
a new body,
and somehow you know you are you.

To All the Mirrored Doors of Beginning

The palimpsest of previous lives
moves us place to place
to all the mirrored doors of beginning,

and then, to the one eternal gateway,
the threshold where God first will see God,
in worlds created to mirror back.

First Self which begat us,
invented death, constant friend,
pushing us forward to live without answers,
as Kierkegard defined:
live life forward, understand backward.

Can that time, the end of the trip,
be that blessed with final knowing?
Reaching closer to the mirrored door,
the entrance by which, one by one,
through the eons we come,
is that same exit through which we depart.

Death, enduring reminder, teases us
with the last promise of finding
the answer to all the whys.

At last, we can take it from this final point,
look backward, understand forward
and we will know.

We Are the Offspring Stardust

Ancient fire, dust, holy water and breath,
passing sacred.

We are the fallout from a secondary star,
swallowed in the miracle
of how we got here,
always mortal fact staring us in the face.

For us, it ends before our matrix.
We die. She lives.

From fiery gusty ocean
evolves our distant beginning's story.

Primeval rocks that soared up,
are tombstones inscribed
with all our nameless names.

The mantra warning
—memento mori—
write your memoir of a living now.

All you get is
now.

Nevertheless

prayers that land nowhere, dead-zoned,
must still be written
with a twig, stick-poked in clay,
or scrawled across a cave,
screamed up to heaven,
or a note tortured into a crevice
of the eternal wailing wall—
those countless entreaties.

God is God is God and gets a lot of messages,
postal code stamped eternity's beginning.
There, God being God, dreams God's God-ness
and eventually reads the mail.

Everything Breathes of God

*Swedish police have allowed the public burning
of sacred Jewish and Christian texts
at a small protest outside Israel's embassy
in Stockholm this Saturday afternoon, July 15th, 2023.*

Everything is one.
So perishingly beautiful.
But always, the always.
What of Evil?
Such a sinner myself, shall I not
have understanding in my heart?

But there is sin and there is sin.
And there are seven heavens,
and four worlds.
But how many hells
for burning God's word?

Education

disappeared,
vanished,
gone like a prayer.

Somewhere perhaps dwells
the necessary educating of oneself
for the journey,
for that last trip—

How to die alone.

The Oldest Person in the Room

that's me—
we are all so terrified of becoming,
to live the tale,
write an ending.

Just be.
Let it happen.

I am an old woman
being born again,
a child starting out
in strange territory.
Yet I feel very young.
Being so old
it all begins one more time,
while the world changes around me.

Into the alone I go
to find out truly who I am,
catch the last,
which is the first moment of truth,
when we are birthed into existence
from the revolving mirrored door
of all beginnings.

Lament for the Crucifixions of October 7

War is upon us.

Sacrificed on the green altar of their pacifist dreams,
they were dancing under a blue sky,
rejoicing in the Torah of joys and continuance,
in a celebration of the life You, God, ordained us to sanctify.
They are crucifixions in the torment
ascending in anguished remembrance, forever and forever.
Their agony endures, lives, lives, lives,
executed by creatures in Your image, *B'Zelem*.

Again, human beasts rise up to annihilate us,
but they are Your creatures, too, no, God?
I have to imagine. Or how did they get here
to this plane of existence, and why?
Will there ever be an answer to that why?

I have lived to this terrible day.
I had hoped to spend this last stretch of being very old
(an unearned gift I must acknowledge),
of an ancient woman, not quite believing she is old,
really old, traveling into the last aloneness,
searching out exalted holy truths before letting go.

Should I persist?
Where shall I find my answers *now*?
I think of Mother Teresa, anguished, who waited and longed,

prayed for God's gone-missing voice to reply to her prayers,
but marched on anyway.

God of us all,
show Yourself, save us again.
You, Lord, God of the Jews,
You, God, that we shared
and gave to this forgetful world.
You, God, Infinite and One. Unknowable.
I ask that the prayers of all the righteous
go to battle for us, since I am not holy enough.
Oh yes, that I most certainly know.
I ask their prayers be heard
that I may ever pray again.

We Are on the Edge of Chaos Again

at the very ledge,
before the deep drop descends into yet another darkly time.
We try to stand ten feet back
to preserve our souls
but we are pushed, pushed
to the catapult
and we must fall
lunging against what will emerge.
Fractals of evil proliferate,
bury us in multiplying horrors.
The fruits of war again, and the whole
is impossibly greater than all the parts.
This cannot stand. A new era begins.

God is still One, and the One is still God.
Living death equals dying life.
Everything started as One.
We all reach the same death
but the equation falls apart at the edge of chaos
and Genesis begins—a new world.

Leonardo DaVinci almost taught us to fly alone.
Perhaps in those secret mirror writings
he wrote down a message he heard from God,
that Adam should have been given wings.
A mistake. A fatal flaw.
Instead, we are like cattle, herded to the edge,
doomed to fall.

Birds are luckier.
Holy as angels
they fly free over all the hells
we make.

This Lament Continues

for all past sweetness.
If I could only write in my soul
the memory of the Sea and the tide swimming back,
soft as washing a newborn infant in a loving murmur,
feeling the cleansing south wind there
when I stood at the ocean
in a kind of holy communion.
And know it all over again.

Once, between my closed eyes,
a purple sun shone in flush glory.
There at the immortal sea,
I perceived a distant mysterium,
veiled in ordained water songs,
when I witnessed the eternity of messages
written in sea braille,
the waves speaking with their every moving drop:
Come. Go back. Return. Forever.
I think I baptized myself
by those waters.
Their faithful return an anointing balm,
a balance, a holy crux
joining my warring souls,
holy water of the holiest.

Standing Over One's Own Grave

at one's foolish last,
takes you cold turkey off artifice.
Period.
Right to the pinpoint of clarity.
That microscopic dot of quantum tininess
which, I understand, is now proven
to be paradoxically infinite.
Meaning, if I could only parse this one out,
there is no Finis to expansion,
no stop to compression.
Nothing really ever ends.
Except somehow us.
But evidently, maybe not.
Death being some kind of trickster of transformation
connected to life, sempiternal, beginning and beginning.
Savage and just. The big Is. And the Big Calm,
in the peace of the graveyard,
ruled by love's resurrecting solace.

Let that be enough.

Sand

1.
Primeval rocks sometimes soar up from oceans
that dry up and vanish with all the nameless names.
We who scratch our moment into petrifying stone,
we live, are no more remembered.
Each grain of sand a story of that shattered rock,
joining all the other erased journeys
in lost infinitudes.

Always the eternal moving,
written in the sands' forbears,
compelled to whittle
rock to smaller rock.
Written in us
to keep moving on
in our own grinding cycle.

Once the sands were solid mass,
ancient godly rock lifted, and placed
as noble altars. Pillars to worship, in that before the before.
There, people somewhat like us
prayed their hopes like us.
Each worshipping stone, each prayer pillar,
now fragmented, transformed, numberless.
Uncountable grains of sand sifted down
the endless hourglass of created time,
journeyed forth by Sea

became the sands that are the beached shores of carpet,
powdered gold in the sun,
a shimmering desert,
sand paintings designing themselves
under the sun's prism glare.

Life begins,
moment by vanishing moment.

2.
By miracle of human cleverness,
we've learned to turn
the harvest of sand barrenness to glass,
look through hidden worlds,
see what we think we see
through mirrored telescopes,
focus on dead universes, while
our own shifting sand is painting stories
that unfold and re-arrange
to points of absolute nothing.

On the sand we see
the miraged oasis ahead.
Our story moves.

What Exactly Are You God?

Truth's origin to find?
The chaos of Infinite Possibilities?
Divine Thought?
Sacred geometrician of fractal reprinting and reprinting
for some reason we can't fathom?
Designer of random outcomes, who dreamed up death,
and fertilization of start-up worlds,
and stories that vanish into black holes of what exactly?

A filament breath passaging us towards the next inch in space?
This much I believe. You are.

You are the absolute Truth.
Instigator of prayers.
Receiver of prayers.

God, why would you need us?
Why do you even want our prayers?
Anyway, I pray to The Unknowable
that I have trouble reaching by prayer,
to The One who
shall be what is already.
I am only a link,
a disappearing inkblot writing my existence
at Your command.

In a Hymn of Sounding Glory

My turn comes.
Welcome bitters.
My past lives gone.
All the strangers I was,
whom I forgive
and even admire.
I was all of them.

Open hinges, gate after gate
let me fly triumphant
through all the cemeteries
of my mind.

God's Endless Confession Booth

When I pray
I get a vision of God's endless confession booth
where myriad conflicting petitioners plead their case,
firmly convinced their cause is being heard.

How awesome and terrifying,
and passing wonderful, miraculous,
to be God present and listening
behind the dividing screen.
And how we feel in all our disunity
we are sometimes answered.

Shall we ever pray together,
enemies trusting each other,
hearing the same message,
given instructions to sin no more,
receiving absolution?
Shall it ever happen?

Standing Near the Edge of Chaos in a Time of War

"What would you like to do,
to be, find your truest self,
to pull yourself back from the ledge?"
asks the therapist to your soul.
"What would be heaven for you now?"

Sticking my foot in the gate before closing time,
clean up all my messes,
leave all love lovingly said,
give what's left for me to give,
say thanks for this moment allotted,
grab harder for the merry-go-round ring
this last time around,
take kinder care of myself
now that I am very old.

Perhaps indulge a healing nap,
paint a poem,
read something awe-inspiring,
remember to breathe deep,
eat some homemade cake,
remember to do what's right,
say aloud to myself what my heart asks,
count the stars in a humbling sky,
acknowledge each monthly moon,
bow in awe before gifted genius,

smile indulgence at others' foibles,
compassion for their sins and mine.
Honor great souls,
have some fun,
clarify my mind,
say what I have to say
and keep it short.
Remember my undeserved good fortune,
pay it forward, give someone else a leg up
and drop a coin in the subway fiddler's hat.
Breathe in white lilacs,
walk child-like in a pelting rain,
dance this solitary last journey with aplomb,
paint joy with an honest brush,
grab the gestural moment
and hold it for all sacred time.
Paint loose on the largest canvas I can find,
befriend that familiar decent stranger
who travels with us to the end.
Live the interesting novel
I haven't got around to being.

Finally, let me just be blessed to witness the utter holiness of peace.
And that will be enough.

Remembering My Dark Funk at the Lovely Beach on a Perfect Day

I should sit quietly,
give it a rest,
sensibly smile my face up into the sun.
The day's cruel headlines intrude
on this glorious beach day
while Something Up There keeps beaming kindly down.

I'm agitating about ordained retribution
for big-time sins.
There may be an answer
just beyond that horizon
where sea and air meet,
that thin line of connection
where the pretty sailboats sit pasted against the sky.

If I could just parse that miracle
of how sea and sky meet,
reach that sacred juncture, understand,
meantime I turn my face up to the sun,
in trust.

Vade Mecum

'Go, come with me.'
A farewell to what must be farewelled.
A handbook to carry to the Mysterion I inevitably join.
Shall I sing praises to oblivion, and the not knowing
in this time of war?
Yes.
There is hope for better,
for the heaven inscribed in heaven.
Where we end being who we were,
emerge into what we are.
Enter God who must have the answers.

Where we don't need to remember anymore.
Just begin.

The Re-Naming of Things

after all is forgotten,
in the garden of old age,
traveling backwards
in the reverse journey
to one's place-mark in the life force.
Going forward that moment
from creation's doorway of beginning,
a continuance that must be named again,
a name needed for that,

or to never return,
from the black pit of the nothing
that needs no name.

We Are Instructed:

'Therefore, choose life'

Here in an evil shadow
of tomorrows that may never come,
if we live, we live God's gift
in the now,

in the sharing of the eternal name
that may not be pronounced,
our present tense occupying
Shall Be What Shall Be—
ordained mystery we share.

How to Die Alone

and kind of nobly,
requires an education of sorts.
Pretty hard to get there stripped,
even without the luggage
dropped along the way.

Perhaps in this evil world
we should wish each other a good death
as the ultimate kindness
so many can't achieve.

Who by this, and who by that?
All the ways death comes, scare me.

How it will happen
we don't know.
God's kiss would be fine.

The Morning Prayer

I thank, with today's perceptions.
I am with and incline myself to Your Presence,
so remote, except only in this—
the continuance I feel,
allotted by You, King, Ruler Supreme,
God of so many Holy Names,
who lives and replenishes all life,
which You return in me
with tenderness,
replacing soul into this flesh
I always take for granted.
You, always faithful to this continuance You began.
Until not.
My days are numbered.

Yet this morning, I was born again from the world of sleep,
from forgotten dreams of unexplained mysteries,
populated by alien dreamers.
That other world which I enter a stranger, every night,
to search my own purpose is why I am there,
to illuminate who I am here, and then awaken.
Almost knowing.
Modah ani. I thank.

There is a Candle in the Dark

of blind hate,
the contaminating shadow
humankind fractals over the planet,
the spidery web of anti-life, death,
and the babel of rationalizing irrationality
hissing its evil song
in the lowest pit
down deep down from the holy ladder above.

A hell is created
in that willed forever of the blackest night
that turns away from the star
that birthed us all,
even in that unholy night of horrors,
there is a candle to kindle.

Coax the flame.
Commemorate God's works.
See each other and ourselves
in the flickering light.

Does the Divine Sensorium of God

participate in the profundity of all our questions,
of why there is anything,
why consciousness,
soul, self, illusion, existence, a beginning, entropy,
continuous disorder, transformation,
a pure energy that won't let go?

Does God care any more about what we think?
We still do.
The first Jews, we Hebrews,
were agnostic in our naming of The Invisible *You*,
a revelation to the world that we haven't been forgiven for yet.
'*What Will Be, Already Is,*
Shall Be What Shall Be.'

Ha Shem who edits our chronicles, our stories,
glass blower artist blowing life,
working in the materials of fiery colliding universes,
painting tapestries from infinity's dust.
To hang up where? And why? Will we ever know?
Does God? Yet? When? With an evolvement from Adam,
a better intelligent design, or just us?
That day, the whole shop will be closed down, the Kabbalists say.
And God will figure out if it was all worth it.

World War Three

It's here. And I have lived to smell it arriving.
War looms. And nobody sees.
I think the worst will plague this earth.

The Kabbalah of inner knowledge is no comfort.
Our warring souls reconciled, no defense.

Tohu v'bohu. Chaos.
Is this the end?

To get it together, figure it out,
be the priestess of useless knowing,
of the terrible and the wonderful and the holy,
all squeezed into the narrow bridge
taking us over the cesspools circling below,
we are commanded to be unafraid of death,
the gift we all discover one way or another.
Others have received the same.

Do the dead commune as they sometimes speak to us in dreams?
Is theirs a holy utterance?
Why do we always feel they have something to tell us?

In the beginning, again and again, forever repeated, the dead return.
Vanished to dust but alive for a while in our heads.
While we live, they live. And when we die, they die.

I am the last of mine.
Again, and again reprieved.
Face it down.
This is our time for war.
Let me exit brave.

Blinding truths descend,
while God is hiding.

The War Against the Jews—Day 86. Israel, Ever Startup Nation Built on Ashes,

lost, finds itself again.
Yet more new beginnings.
We are climbing Jacob's ladder of the promised dream.
Our navigational third eye buried tight
in a chest of grief.
Choosing to climb ahead, we, Your chosen, choose again
the forward desert sojourn,
carrying the Ark of Our Commitment
through all the battles connected with Your promised land
of milk and honey and sweet justice
for which we must fight like animals
to ward off animals also made in Your image.
In a world happy to scapegoat us,
into what wilderness left? Where to hide?
There is no escaping, fight or be finished,
before we continue up that ladder to whatever Your purpose.
This is war. Day 86.

When can new start-up nation miracles burst forth
for those ingrates twittering on their cell phones
operating courtesy of Jewish brains
and cursing Israel to destroy us utterly.
Plainly, we have few friends
in those who arrogated You from our first Covenant
and try to write us out of history.

God, keep us strong
with whatever cunning of desperation, we need.
Of all your creatures, we are alone.
Instruct us how to navigate this shrinking world
with Your two tablets, the ten ordaining laws
no one thanks us for.
If we must flee, where shall we go?
One ever-disputed dot of a place
You granted us, comes accompanied
by war and war and war. Shed blood.
A foe at every border.

Yet, facing our enemies this time again,
we choose. Your people live.
We choose to be us. *Am Yisrael Chai.*

Day 88

How pray to the Owner of all mysteries beyond?
When order exists in disorder except for humankind.
Are You even with us on this journey anymore?
Reveal Yourself to us on these killing grounds of desecrations.

We stand, the shattered remnant of Your abiding truths,
defenders of Your ancient laws inscribed
in those sacred scrolls of continuance written without vowels,
our stubborn enchiridion of commandments,
a holy vanished conversation of dialogues recorded in heaven,
spoken in a dialect long forgotten,
that we decipher, word by holy word,
parsing each day's message from Your eternal Torah,
preserved by our—Your martyred faithfuls.

Save us, Lord. As we defend You.

The Hostages. Day 88 of the Unspeakable

Hear that prayer we have pleaded
through the ages,
Your children, hostages again and again.
Chosen for?
Bring Them Home.
And if they are mercifully dead,
let them rise to Your heights,
scale all the seven heavens
through all the dimensions
till they reach Your throne.
Let there be a heaven above all heavens
and let there be recompense for the unspeakable done.
Let there be a meaning in all the meaningless.
Let this all be for something.

These Are the Messages Writing Themselves Out

on the wall that divides:

World War Three Is Here.

The malignant hydra deities of war
beat the drums of carnage:

Carry a gun!

This time we carry a gun.

Lament

How shall I *ever* pray to You again
in the short time remaining to me?
How shall I ever pray again?

The very old should die
ahead of the freshest horrors,
give pious comfort to those who must proceed.

Shall the old be blessed and comfortable
living too long?
Seems we must suffer too in our disbelief
of Your kindness to the innocent,
to the true of heart.

Let evil be recompensed.
I want to meet You with trust,
with a sanctification,
with a bending to holiness,
with a rapture of beauty,
with a hallelujah.

Let me not whimper my last in despair.
Let me find You magnificent,
glorious, the answer to all my questions.

Kabbalah

I try to draw the living tree
ascending to that place
where we all begin.
Ah, searching holiness
in this garbage-laden world,
me and my tribe
traversing all the sewers of hate
each step on the rung,
and asking God why.
Another and another why,
why continue?

And if not,
a deeper terrifying why.
Why even ask?
But if not,
then what?
And why, ever at all,
the whole of it?

Gnarled Old Tree

OMG.
I am travelling down this avenue of ancient trees
planted when the street's occupants were young as I.
And now, how mighty against the grey winter sky
these old trees stand, naked in their wonder,
reaching up to life,
crooked, bent every which way,
abstract drawings, towering, flailing out in courage.

O you gnarled, beloved, recent friend,
I, being now one of your company,
aspire to your triumphing majesty.
Your glory inspires me.

Bent and moving,
I discover I am you:
another gnarled tree of amassed mystery,
conundrum to my very own self,
praying to earn wisdom in this dying forest.
One by one,
our lessons done; we leave.

But not yet, me.

Future Evolve

Someday perhaps we shall learn to fly.
Soar. Float through the ether
of all our ancient dreams.
We will be creatures of infinite peace.
Evolved creations of God.
Reaching to the Hand
that creates us,
over and over,
joined
and at home in heaven's sky.

We will travel with angels,
with all those who have watched over our shoulders.
We will arrive to Nirvana. To *Moksha*.
To the end that will be the end.
No more beginning. Nothing.
The story written.
Finis.

Experimental Flaw

O Perfect in Imperfections,
weaving in the flaw
that morphs to black hole evils,
You, Author of all our miseries,
of all our holiest exaltations,
why?
Always the why. Why begin this stuff
if You already know all the possible endings
living with and in each of us.
Your voice of consciousness I feel in me,
is in that man, the Hamas creature
who craves to kill me
with dimensionless cruelties.
He also calls out a sacred name for You,
who lives in both our breaths.
He is my blood enemy of unholy wars,
in whom You exist as surely as You occupy me.
How is it that You enact Your Grand Passion
of what is to come and become, through us?
Or do we anymore populate your grand opus?
Maybe You long ago scratched us off
into Your galactic wastebasket of failed scenarios
and somewhere in Eternity,
have written a better script with a stellar cast
performing Your dream of becoming what must become:
the *"I shall be what I shall be."*
Meantime, for most of us,

You Still Are
as we inch our lives forward and back to You,
who placed us here.

If This is the First Day and the Last Day of My Life, How Shall I Proceed?

How can I even start this day with a praying poem?
Because today again war continues.
Every morning, we wake up with wars.
And now another bigger war is here.
I know it.

Because I am so near the end I suppose, is why
I am privileged to see this crazed delivered message
blood-streaked across the computer screen,
on the TV, on my I-phone, headlining the morning paper,
tossed down at my door.
A crackle of paper announcing dread.

I try to conjure God's opinion about the necessity of war
in some Eternal Plot, the originating blueprint novel of novels,
the manuscript that directs us to The End.
God's voice, a doubt and a taunt, is me, ghost-writing in my head
and for sure being no Moses, I still have the effrontery to write down
what I figure could be God's monologue (if I were that August Presence):

"I realize myself in all of you my creatures
I am you and you and you,
I am The One,
Singing in all your veins
enemy against enemy,
I am The One in The Everything.

In you, I traverse epoch by epoch.
And I let be chosen
the Who of my substance that shall endure.
The Me Who Will Bless
at Eternity's last fork in the road,
the Me That Must Continue,
the Me That Will Read the final script,
that will Choose the last path to unite
all My Selves cell by inchoate cell.
And I, Supreme though I Be,
shall finally know why I created
humankind and never stopped when things were good,
after planting the sublime trees in My sacred garden.
Why was I so lonely to create Adam?
Still luckily did invent Death to move things along."

Of course, this is all my head talking,
and I can't hear a thing from above
except my own ideas forming.
Once upon a time, I could really pray,
sense an answer, an echo to my need, a deep sound.
I felt pure Holiness. The hearing of me.

Gone, absent that feeling of The Presence,
I commune with myself, imagining
God's Fatal Flaw and other absurdities,
declaring I won't accept the invention of bottomless evil.

This can't be the only scenario. What for?
This remains my stubborn question directed above
or wherever direction it should be aimed.
We are stuck in a script that doesn't seem to work
until, presumably, the One on High gets it right.
And unfortunately, incumbent upon us is
our constant itching search to move things along.

World War Three?
What's another war in the larger scheme of things?
The glory of all the heavens will continue.
We die anyway. But no. I declare no,
my dissatisfaction and my objection.
I will kill my enemy before he kills me.

Shall I sing a victory hymn,
a Hosanna, to the God who lives in both of us?

If This Is the Last Day of My Life, How Shall I Proceed?

I am so very old
and the old should die on a nice note of hope.
I know how it feels when your world suddenly collapses,
dies at your feet and you are defenseless.

War. War. War. The war continues. I have lived to witness war again.

We Jews have documented ourselves in wars.
Tanach is our Jewish trajectory of war upon war.
All the other wars registered in history books, no one reads anymore.
Each time after war, our civilizations changed.
Evolved. Evolving. Only through wars.
Is this the ruling law of existence?
Wars. Someone wins. Many die. Many suffer.

This earthy existence, panoply tapestry,
woven with human plots that hit the divine wastebasket. Pulverized.
But earth's natural story is written in fossils we can decipher,
towering mountains we can climb,
a geography of the dead and continuing alive that we can still read.

Human stories are dead and gone
as the newsprint that wrapped the fish and chips
in the extinct fish shop around the corner.
All that print age's moldering journalism,
that glorious fish wrap,

now transformed to social media grunts,
soon to be lost to more plundering technological change
that will evaporate into holograms and puff into nothing.

Maybe we'll leave a bone.
Eons pass and all our clever words vanish.
What will we ever communicate to dead stars?
Where even is the message sent to us?
Transcribed and lost.
Once we stood below the holy mountain.
We heard. We saw.
The memory, we carried bosom to bosom and carry now.

If for no other reason, I better pray
that all the sacred scrolls endure
because once upon a time
the soul wrote on holy parchment,
reached on High
when our world was young and growing.

If this is my last day
with what true holy words shall I proceed?
Well, Death, you seem to be teaching me.
before you snatch it all away.
How Shall I Proceed?

O Lord, Master of All, how do you measure Your time?
The passing circuits of galaxies,
the panorama of disintegrating universes.
Is there even a meaning to Time?
Do you measure in quantum disappearance?
Do You, with us, count time
by moving moons, gravitating suns, eon days?
Live and resurrect happily in all your rotating creations,
amazingly, in us.
Rise up, resurge in life immortal till it is not.

Rebirth and rebirth.
Beyond counting. Beyond division.

Teach me to pray for my children.
Though I myself, did not want to arrive here,
I do not want to leave,
yet now leaving, I can only bless those who enter,
also unwilling, screaming into the light.
May they be spared to bless existence,
re-climb the ladder once more
to Your Mirrored Door of Beginnings,
to infinite expanding visions,
to initial incubating joys, Hallelujah.

If This Is the Last Day

then I need focus,
zero in to all the beginnings
which spell out the end.

First and always is
that Eternal Last Question:
'*What was it all worth
gathering up what you did
under the sustaining sun?*' *(Ecclesiastes)*

My generation goes,
your future comes
and this earth we inherit stands for a while,
spinning itself to eternity
while the sun rises, departs,
returns forward to its incipient glory
and eventual flaming death.

I study this last prayer,
grasped from all our befores,
from that unnamed son of David,
from the many who have re-written the singing words:
There is a season, a time given to you
under all the heavens
to approach and taste heaven below.
There was a time for you to be born
and there is a time for you to die.

You should have learned not to waste the time between.
A time to plant rightly
and to savor what you pull up from its roots.
A time to kill if you must.
Kill or be eaten and the law of the sea
and the churning cycle of earth.
A time to heal a bird's broken wing.
A time to break down the walls that time would erode.
A time to build another world.
A time to weep out your very kishkas.
And a time to laugh through your gut.
A time to wail blue murder. Mourn.
And a time to dance it off.

A time for throwing stones?
I am not so sure about that.
I'd rather gather them up.

A time to embrace with deepest abandon.
A time to refrain.
A time to search out meanings
and a time to be totally lost.
A time to preserve as holy,
and a time to let it all go.
A time to rip apart
and a time to sew together.
A time for silence
and a time to speak out.
A time for love
and a time for hate.
A time for war
and in this unholy time,
a time for peace.

We are waiting.

Shoah

Never would I believe
I would wail a lament
for the suffering living
and rejoice for those safely dead.
Six months since October 7,
that Hamas-abominated day
when they took our people hostage.
We can't sound out the names still alive.
One by one, they have been cursed beyond hope.
In cages, the women abused as no animal ever has.
Shall I pray for them to live? Endure?

Why have I lived to this age
in health and remaining prospects?
If not able to sing in last joy
a hymn to everything good,
instead, I must curse the pure evil
descending on us,
every minute of hell perpetrated from Hamas-religious minds.
We are forced to write the dirge that howls up to accuse You, God.
For what did You require of them in religion, their clean-feet prayers?
And why given no detailed promise of punishment beyond the grave,
instead of 72 virgins rewarding sick meditations on jihad?

So much for the steady philosophical climb
up Jacob's ladder of abstract understanding,

I want to believe in a flaming future hell,
real hellfire, the works.
Let us all be punished for our sins.
Let Hamas burn forever and forever,
tongue tattooed with each searing name
of the living martyrs of October 7.
Let Hamas burn in the infinite cauldron hells
of all the universes.
Yes. This is a time to believe in hell.
Or nothing.

Make My Peace

in God's waiting room,
that special place I am privileged to occupy
at ninety-five years.
I cannot go on forever.
This life must end.

Let me write the final passage
with hope for my children
and yes, hope for all my dead
residing with me now in my mind.
While I exist, so do they,
but till when?
Do they die with me?

Lou, I Held Your Hand

and felt your comfort of me as you were leaving.
Your sudden strength gave me courage
as I tried to ease you over into that place
where I am not sure we will ever again meet.
You were my friend until that very moment
when you knew death was coming for you.
That's my last memory of you.
That somehow, I gave you power to depart,
perhaps gave you one last moment of happiness.

Now I am the last of the last,
speaking to all my dead
since they can no longer speak to me.
I shall enter their silence.

And so, I speak to myself.
The dead are dead.
I am still alive, far from deathbed words
and yet close.
Let this be a prayer,
a guiding protection for all those I will leave behind.
Let my heart, my soul
be this pressing hand blessing you forever.
Amen.

Last Messages: The Writing on The Wall in a Time of War

that we, the old despair to read:
The story is closing,
We may not get to see the end
of all the woes descending on those we leave behind,
how things turn out.

One foot in God's waiting room,
we live. And that must be enough.

In My 96th Year

I am obsessed
to search out the truth of all things,
to see the picture clear
before I go as go I must.

Traveling to that last frontier
to the truth of one's own self,
which is?
Can it ever be the truth of all things
or just my one small truth
that dies into the dust of the only reality—
time's one-way clock?

Oh God, I realize I may stir up again
as a worm, here in the circling wheel of earth life,
knowing and not knowing all over again.

When all I want to know is the why of the truth
and the truth of the why, but can't find it,
and if I do get it full jolt to my forehead,
I would be in agony of ecstasy,
or in deep gut moral pain.

Still, I search, but
clever bastard animals some humans are,
how glean this need to know?
A digital photo lies.

The digital word lies.
The greatest minds lie,
politicians of course,
and ourselves, too, mostly.

In 2024, to obliterate
any historical record of truths,
we have influencers,
embodiments of the big, bigger, biggest ever lie.

Let us somewhere find Cassandras,
fiery prophets foaming at the mouth
spitting burning embers of the truths of all the stars,
of hell fires; but better,
a seventh heaven's golden glow
and a toasted perfect marshmallow tossed
from God's holy bonfire.

Just give me one midnight-blue holy night
where I can look up and be thrilled
by infinity's trillions of stars,
the everything of everything
and let me float out to meet them,
into the "is" that is,
the truth that is the judgement of God, the ineffable,
the Final Judge
Who shall instruct.

Full Circle

I think this is where I came in.
I instruct myself in this latter time
of descending strangling evils,
a world set to go on fire
as has happened to so many before me,
rudely shocking better people.

Knowing too much and knowing too little,
I approach the mirrored door of beginning
from where I exited ninety-five years ago,
when I knew just how to proceed
in every neutron and atom,
a born master of beginnings,
but in my case, sadly I can only imagine
the resultant bitterly un-requited hopes I engendered,
because every birth augurs again
the arrival of some kind of messiah.
So, mother, father, sorry about the inevitable letdown
I presented to your expectations.
Anyway, here I am.

'*Futility of Futilities. All is futile*"

This aging process of return facing me smack in the face
involves the hard slog
taken up by all the past doomsayers of meaninglessness,
arrived at by varied consensus of the wisest of the wisest,
decade after decade, an eon of generations, till today.

Even that clever bunch couldn't get a handle on it.
Dying, that is, its prospect, the process whereby and the rotten conclusion
that nothing is reliable but death squatting in a corner of your mind
reminding that you haven't figured out any grand answer
to carry you through the inevitable,
the price you have to pay for living.
Always The Ending. A Last Curtain Call, if you're lucky. And finis.
I can't yet face graciously letting go.
Like most everyone else on this planet,
I am cursed to die with all my questions unresolved.
Did I hang around too long?
Seeing as our Jewish golden age is over,
it's time for us all to move on. But where?
And how inconvenient to leave before
we see how this latest war turns out.
And how can I, like all those before me,
leave my children hostages to the same damned fate
that has eaten up our very flesh
from the bonfires of the Inquisition
to infants tortured in the oven hellfire of October Seven.

Where will you go my children?
I thought I could protect you.
I have been doomed to grow old in this particular, world-wide war,
evil chaotic time of empires hitting the dirt once more
and I, foolish trusting mother, have trapped you here, my loves,
just by giving you life.
I shall return to where you entered,
to that very place where you, too, shall return.
Blows my mind.
Death escorts us all back to where dying is the one and only entry fee
to some possible explanation waiting
at our entrance point to all the beginnings.

If it's even an issue or a possibility,
if we have any say in the decision made,

I would like to hold off on future incarnations.
God, if You be God, instruct me how to avoid
coming back here in future wars. Be with me,
let me return to a time of redeemed glory,
another golden era under an embracing sun,
or teach me the purpose of the wars
you write in the DNA of this our earthly sojourn.
I don't want to leave with the curse of
All is futile as a last message to my children.
I want there to be a future after this war,
for my people, for a doomed world.
Be with your creatures, God,
our rock of all the ages past and to come, be God.

Mirrored in Your enigmatic design,
let me learn what we all must learn
to earn that entrance fee we all must pay.
Teach me in time how to leave.

I Will Go Out Fighting

as long as I can.
Tilt against all my foolish windmills.
I am that I am as surely God,
as You Are What You Are.

Cursed with understanding
and still a working brain,
I will not say I am blessed to see this day,
but I will not go out meekly.

Here I stand, ready to study more and more
of the world's hate,
the sequels to Hitler dooming our planet.

I will do battle till I cannot.
This shall be my final doing
until I cannot do it anymore.

Today my brain is clear,
and if it remains so
I pledge it to this final fight of my life.
Let me die an old soldier
joining the very young dying
in all the senseless wars ever fought.

This War of Wars and More Futile Quarrels with God

A sea of Jew-hate is upon us now.
Shall You allow it to drown our souls?
Again, and again and again,
since that time on the mountain,
when You spoke and we, standing below, heard.
And ever since we got chosen
for the cryptic, moving message,
You choose us.

Lord of infinite fractal infinities, Your
originating fractal erupted from Your solitary root.

You choose us, invent us,
to propel your message forth,
to decode the writing on Your eternal wall of change.
We, Your choosing Chosen.
The world persecutes us.
We few remain.

Can You move forward without us?
Why must we always be Your catalyst—
the yeasty starter of the eternal bread of strife?
On this planet of eat or be eaten
we live on the ashes of death.
Do You feed on us, require, depend on us
to move Your Adam experiment forward?

The next development in this laboratory of surprise concoctions,
forming what You had in mind
when You blueprinted the grand idea,
the singing story elucidating what You Need to Be
in order to see Yourself in us at infinity's end?
Can it really be true we are essential to Your plan?

You choose us in particular,
to act out Your mysteriously strange need of us.
On this planet, Your people, the ordained scapegoat.
Jews, Jews, Jews,
forever and forever, are the world's news.
It seems this planet can't do without us.

Again, and again.
Choosing us,
we few stubborn who choose You
again, and again
are sanctified in pure stubbornness,
each of us an invention
in the world's hating mind.
If we didn't exist, we would have to be made up.

Every living, warring thing breathes of You, God.
The Yang dot in the Yin, the Yin dot in the Yang.
And the one who comes to kill me exults
his name for You on his lips.

Do you exist in all the religions we make
on this failed planet?
Are we forever doomed, ordained, blessed
to execute Your plan?
Without *Jews*, can that be done?
Remember Lord,
the everlasting Covenant we made.

Be with Your people.

From a Dinosaur Evolved a Soaring Bird

that flies with God,
communing in song,
in choirs of rapture roaming
sky's blue cathedral.

Traveling with a Godly message inscribed —
exquisite, passages through the heavens,
singing with the angels
if any creature ever did,
with wings taking it across worlds.

A bird is a holy creature
free to fly from its own hell.
Butterflies are free. Even flying bats.

With wings embedded
we should have flown to Heaven's door,
arrived to God's delight
and with the angels, joined in God's grace.
Alas.

All the Journeys' Ends Are New Beginnings

So, it is written, forever and forever.
On death's ashes new life stirs.

We die. Another begins.
In times of so rare peace
there is a certain, blessed calm
found in the moldering graveyard
where we aged can contemplate our own inscribed headstone,
feel graced to write its final message,
comforted that we shall only hear the clod
descending on our own caskets.

Mashber, The Birthing Stool of Crisis

Day 176.
We are splayed
torn apart
into the throes of a birth
that looms as the spewing forth of a monster
who will usher in World War 3.
Our enemies, the cruelest ever known,
promise horrors to come.

Or
this our world's warring womb
may burst open to an inchoate renaissance climbing
up Jacob's ladder to a world of continuance
and we humans shall surely reach those furthest stars
before eternity closes shop.

All our holy books are a litany of wars and outcomes,
improvement upon improvement, honed
on the rough instruments of battle.
That's the story so far.
But what refinements work on nuclear bomb explosions?

It is told to us in the Torah so matter-of-factly:
"When you go out to war. . ." then the rules of conduct follow.

What are the rules when your enemy is
Hitler's resurrected bastard child beloved of an evil world?
Then what shall we do?

Do you, reader, know how to speak with God?
Then discuss this with HER and never stop.

May the prayers of the righteous reach God's ear.

Old Age Must Live with Not Knowing

The end of the novel started,
the outcome of this cursed war,
who your great grandchildren will become,
if and how the world will fall apart
in global warming,
earth blood-soaked,
or nuclear bombed.
Anyway, you'll be gone.

Every night, know this for sure—
a visit from the angel of death
is reasonable expectation.

Here and now arrives this final time to think about goodbyes,
plus giving a paean of thanks for whatever
ordained and sustained us this time around,
(Supposing we were here before)
if not, then our last time ever,
seeing as there won't be anything more.

Is it so terrible to die?
Billions of times before,
in this divine sensorium of existence
of absolute wonder and thudding horror,
this dance of life and death
and consciousness extinguished
has happened before.

Is there more?
At the end, do we find out why something is,
instead of nothing
and what our purpose signified:
why we lived,
why we died,
why we hoped,
why we were,
why we loved.
Only to lose it all.

The only thing I know for sure, right now,
my story ends.
I can only hope death smiles kind for me
here in my good luck of stubborn age
where I live on,

while the young die brave
and some live caged in the same Hamas hell
where their enemy rots in ruins.

Let me live to reach the day
when all the young are free and reckless in their hopes,
a day perhaps of any kind of peace,
the end of this war
and everyone's children singing,
and that will be enough.

Unicursal Labyrinth

According to Wikipedia
a unicursal labyrinth has only one single path to the center
and presents no navigational challenge.
This solves my dilemma completely.
I see clearly where I'm going.
I need only thread my way forward
for as long as the road takes me.
I shall not get lost.
Wherever I stop, the journey's made.

IS

The present tense, *Hoveh*
lives in the middle of God's holy name.
Past, present, future.
Was. Is. Shall Be.

For a while we travel in the now,
trapped
moving forward.
One can only conclude
that God moves forward too,
having invented relentless Time.

What was before the cosmic clock got sent ticking,
the same sublime spectral nothingness
we enter when death calls our name?
What is now?

Perhaps we shall find out.
Perhaps we shall not.

Form Returns to Formlessness

As we began, so we continue, so we end,
each, our journey.

Ajoining together, a growing—
earth greening and sprouting,
bursting alive, and more alive,
each cell, atom, neutron, spreading,
searching, finding its place.
We are built for climactic love
and giving birth to continuance,
the glory moment fulfilled,
form achieved,
body completed,
fullness. The peak.

Then starts our return to formless energy,
with the divine Qi guiding us
back to the invisible spark
that brought us out of nothingness,
divine mystery that cannot be solved,
the beginning of beginning.

We reach the drop curtain
that must be pulled down
on our small stage,
the place where we stand
and then not, moving on
to our uncharted final destination.

Along that last path,
we hope to nobly navigate
the breaking down,
the coming apart.

As Qi life force travels backwards
through our veins, our flesh, our being,
inching towards the ticking clock,
timed to complete our passage
from form that is us,
to the falling apart into the dust
of all that is fated past residue,
there, a newly empty terrain waits
for another worm of beginning.
We go to that nothing
perhaps to be implanted
with holy sparks of continuance.
Who are we, exactly,
when we are no more?

The Garden Breathes into Winter

does not die,
gathers up peace.

Coda to a Bitter Story Unfolding

PARTING BLESSINGS, AS I LEAVE—

May the truth and beauty of your childhood soul follow and be with you all the days of a long life full of purpose, meaning, and true love, under the canopy of God's benevolent presence.

May you wake up from dreams that connect you to your truest self.

May you be blessed to meet and be joined in long, happy companionship with your fated chosen one.

May you exult in good health and in the knowledge of how to maintain your body.

May you be blessed with abundance to share.

May you turn challenges into victories.

May every loss be softened with the ongoing love of a company of dear ones.

May you be blessed by fate.

May you keep a compassionate heart and have the luck to meet equally compassionate souls in your life journey.

May you learn wondrous things, may you never stop studying the miracles of this existence.

May you never be lonely for long.

May you be blessed with many friends and be counted as a true friend.

May you relish your own company and solitude.

May you be fortunate enough to achieve discernment and understanding through teachers and become a preceptor yourself of higher truths.

May you be true to your truest self.

How Beautiful the World Could Be. And is.

In a world of the horrors some make
let it stay shining in its glory for you.
Full of promise in each morning's new hope,
a sustaining prayer you carry with strength.
A warrior of all the burgeoning goods
you weave through your every minute,
a shield against the evils that come,
as you travel Jacob's ladder upward, be
blessed and blessed and blessed.

May you be blessed and guided to make the decisions you won't regret.

May these my parting blessings stand guard against those who curse you.

IF GOD IS IN THE EVERYTHING, AND IS

then our deaths, and we
are in God imploding—
The Oneness all tangled up.
God dies with us and rises
again and again, inchoate,
beginning forever.

God trying everything out:
How to be a songbird.
How to be a cockroach.
A cuttlefish. How to be in its own image
in the created necessary dance
confronting implanted evil
that keeps things rolling
in the self-smitten dance of life.

Sometimes, God, You hold
our child hands in sweetness.

Be with us.

Tree Artist Has Burst Out Wild and Fast, This June. It is Day 261 of War.

Imprinter of the magic code
that resurrects each dead flower's return,
has painted green and green and green,
lush and lush and lush,
a saturate leaf mass greenness
against sky's endless purest blue,
crowning tender sapling branches
and the gnarled old bark of ancient trees.

All those heroes of winter,
maddened contortions flailing out,
sculptures of defiance,
are now canopied in glory.
Their world of tree-speaking-to-tree
exhales anointing perfumes, healing calm.

God,
there, in all the greenness.
Holiness of life. Blesses itself.

O God, bless us too.

Glossary

Adam Kadmon	Primordial Man.
Am Y'Israel Chai	The People of Israel live.
B'Zelem	In God's Image.
Four Worlds	Kabbalah concept of four spiritual worlds—Emanation, Creation, Formation and Action.
Ecclesiastes	Attributed to Koheleth, Son of David. (9th century BCE)
HaShem	The Name. God. Hebrew.
Hoveh	Present Tense of Hebrew.
Kabbalah	Mystical interpretation of the bible.
Kishkas	Literally, stomach/gut, Yiddish
Mashber	Birth, breaking forth, from *Shabar*, Hebrew.
Moksha	Release. Liberation. Sanskrit
Modah Ani	'I thank'. Hebrew.
Mysterion	Mystery rite. Greek
Qi	Circulating life force. Literally, 'Air, breath'. Mandarin.
Seventh Heaven	The highest heaven where God and the most exalted angels dwell. Kabbalah.

Shoah   The mass murder of Jews under the German Nazi regime during the period 1941–45. The Holocaust. Modern Hebrew. Literally, 'catastrophe'.

Tohu v'bohu   Formless chaos, void. Hebrew. Literally, an 'empty desert', expressing the primordial state of the universe before creation.

Vade Mecum   Literally "go with me', modern Latin.

www.ingramcontent.com/pod-product-compliance
Lightning Source LLC
Chambersburg PA
CBHW061455040426
42450CB00007B/1364